GW01459671

If anybody ever asks you, "What religion is it?" you may answer, "Sufism is the religion of the heart; the religion in which one thing is most important and that is to seek God in the heart of mankind."

–Pir-o-Murshid Hazrat Inayat-Khan

Sufi Tales for Children

One Love, One Light

AS TOLD BY Hazrat Inayat-Khan

ILLUSTRATIONS BY STEPHANIE REYES

All rights reserved.

Source material in the text courtesy of Suluk Press an imprint of Omega Publications, Motilal Banarsidass Publishers, and Shambhala Publications

Winged-Heart calligraphy courtesy of Hafizullah Chishti

NURANI KIDS
An imprint of Al-Mukhtar Books

© 2015 Nurani Kids

Library of Congress Control Number: 2015904439
ISBN: 978-0-9831488-5-2

Printed in the United States of America and the United Kingdom.

DEDICATION

This children's book is dedicated to my Sheikha, Amat-un-Nur, whose *words flow as the sacred river*, and to our Pir, whose hand is over the group. May God accept this work and make it an ongoing charity *(sadaqat al-jariya)* for the compiler's father, Gregory S. Grimes.[i]

My Lord, have mercy upon them,

as they raised me up when I was little.

(Qur'an, 17:24)

EPIGRAPH

We read in the Hindu scriptures that: "Truth is One; men call it by various names."

We read in the Buddhist scriptures that: "All things are made of one essence, yet things are different according to the forms which they assume under different impressions." [ii]

We read in the Zoroastrian scriptures that: "Verily, I believed Thee, O Ahura Mazda,[iii] to be the supreme benevolent Providence, for I beheld Thee as the Primeval Cause of all creation."

We read in the Hebrew scriptures that: "The Lord our God, the Lord is One."

We read in the Christian scriptures that: "I and the Father are One."[iv]

We read in the Islamic scriptures that: "Our God and your God is but One and we obey Him alone."

CONTENTS

Once a wise guardian was asked by a child, 'But is it a real story?' and he said, "As a story it is real."

— Pir-o-Murshid Hazrat Inayat-Khan

COMPILER'S NOTE

Dear parents,

Sufi Tales for Children: One Love, One Light is a compilation of stories drawn from the works of the eminent musician and mystic of the early twentieth century, Hazrat Inayat-Khan (1882-1927). This book focuses on the first principal of Sufism, namely, "There is One God, the Eternal, the Only Being; none exists save He."[v] Over a century ago, Hazrat Inayat-Khan brought Sufism from his native India to the West, and left us with a stirring commentary on this principal and a number of classic tales to illustrate his point, such as the story of Khwaja 'Usman Harvani and his foremost disciple Khwaja Gharib Nawaz, the account of Moses and the peasant boy, as well as the debate between a Brahmin and an iconoclast, among others.

This book has five main divisions: the first focuses on Hazrat Inayat-Khan's main thesis, God is One and Lord of all, which is brought to life in tales I-V, the next section features three stories that teach us how to see the Lord, our God, through someone else's eyes (VI-VIII), the third section takes us *toward the One* (IX), whilst the fourth imparts the importance of spiritual courtesy which is, in fact, the root of spiritual liberty (X). The final section plants the seed of liberation, the desire to yearn for the One in this life itself (XI). Each division is preceded by a scripture verse, prophetic tradition, and a mystical poem.

When speaking about the education of children, Hazrat Inayat-Khan observed that stories were the best way for a child to absorb ideals; he also noted that stories told in early childhood remain with the child throughout his or her life.[vi] For young children who delight in being read to, these tales are a means for the family to partake in the great blessing of communion. But this work is also intended for those who are children at heart, who will undoubtedly be delighted by the wit, wisdom, and universal message of Hazrat Inayat-Khan and his principal Sufi thought.

The compiler's intention is to "spread the knowledge of unity, the religion of love and wisdom."[vii]

– Maryam Qadri

INTRODUCTION

By Hazrat Inayat-Khan

There are ten principle Sufi thoughts, which comprise all the important subjects with which the inner life of man is concerned. [This children's book focuses on the first thought, *"There is One God, the Eternal, the Only Being; none exists save He."*]

The God of the Sufi is the God of every creed, and the God of all. Names make no difference to him. Allah, God, *Gott, Dieu, Khuda, Brahma,* or *Bhagwan,* all these names and more are the names of his God; and yet, to him, God is beyond the limitation of name. He sees his God in the sun, in the fire, in the idol which diverse sects worship; and he recognizes Him in all the forms of the universe, yet knowing Him to be beyond all form; God in all, and all in God, He being the Seen and the Unseen, the Only Being. God to the Sufi is not only a religious belief, but also the highest ideal the human mind can conceive.

The Sufi, forgetting the self and aiming at the attainment of the divine ideal, walks constantly all through life in the path of love and light. In God the Sufi sees the perfection of all that is in the reach of man's perception and yet he knows Him to be above human reach. He looks to Him as the lover to his beloved, and takes all things in life as coming from Him, with perfect resignation. The sacred name of God is to him as medicine to the patient. The divine thought is the compass by which he steers the ship to the shores of immorality. The God-ideal is to the Sufi as a lift by which he raises himself to the eternal goal, the attainment of which is the only purpose of his life.[viii]

Sufi Tales for Children

One Love, One Light

Truly those who believe, and those who are Jews, and the Christians, and the Sabeans – whosoever believes in God and the Last Day and works righteousness shall have their reward with their Lord. No fear shall come upon them, nor shall they grieve.

– Qur'an, 2:62

"The prophets are paternal brothers; their mothers are different, but their religion is one."

– Prophet Muhammad

The face of each beauty is the reflection of His face;
The fragrance and color of each garden are His.
In every heart and soul, the search for Him alone;
Every tongue and every mind, His thought adorns.
The goal of every creed and religion is His abode;
He is the ultimate aim of every sect and nation.
In the Ka'ba, in the church and in the temple,
The worshippers are entranced by His eyes.

– Shah Niaz

THE TALE OF TWO SUFIS

There was a great Sufi teacher in India who had a thousand adherents who were most devoted pupils. One day he said to them, "I have changed my mind." And the words "changed my mind" surprised them greatly; they asked him, "What is the matter, how can it be that you have changed your mind?" He said, "I have the feeling that I must go and bow before the goddess Kali." And these people, among whom were doctors and professors, well qualified people, could not understand this whim, that their great teacher in whom they had such faith wished to go into the temple of Kali and bow before the Goddess of the hideous face, he, a God-realized man in whom they had such confidence! And the thousand disciples left

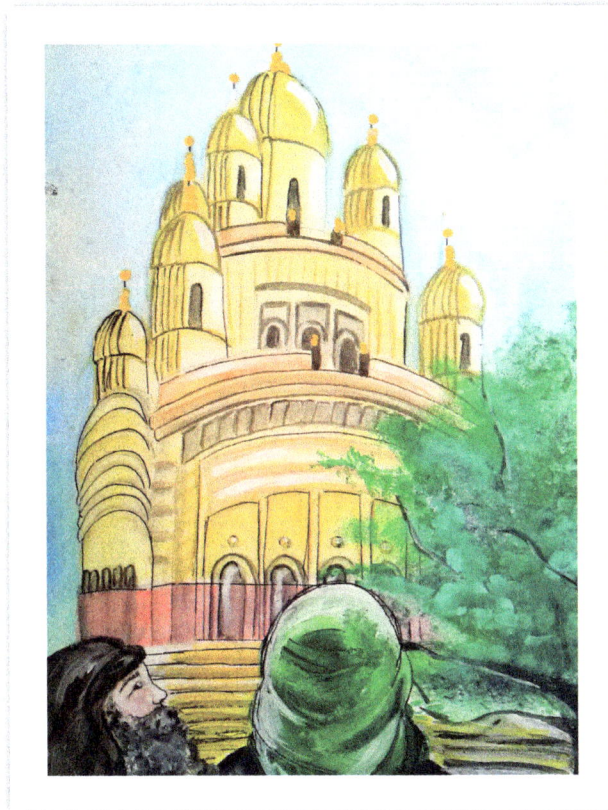

him at once, thinking "What is this? It is against the religion of the formless God, against the teaching of this great Sufi himself that he wants to worship the goddess Kali!"

And there remained only one pupil, a youth who was very devoted to his teacher, and he followed him when he went to the temple of Kali. The teacher was very glad to get rid of these thousand pupils, who were full of knowledge, full of their learning, but who did not really know him; it was just as well that they should leave. And as they were going toward the temple, he spoke three times to this young man, saying "Why do you not go away? Look at these thousand people, who had such faith and such admiration, and now I have said just one word, and they have left me. Why do you not go with them? The majority is right." The pupil, however, would not go, but continued to follow him. And through all this the teacher received great inspiration and a revelation of how strange human nature is, how soon people are attracted and how soon they can fly away. It was such an interesting phenomenon for him to see the play of human nature that his heart was full of feeling, and when they arrived at the temple of Kali he experienced such ecstasy that he fell down and bowed his head low. And the young man who had followed him did the same.

When he got up he asked this young man again, "Why do you not leave me when you have seen a thousand people go away? Why do you follow me?" The young man answered, "There is nothing in what you have done that is against my convictions, because the first lesson you have taught me was that nothing exists save God, there is nobody else except God before whom to bow, even in bowing before Kali. It was the first lesson you taught me." All these learned men were given the same lesson, they were students and very clever, but they could not conceive of that main thought which was the center of all the teaching. It was this same young man who later became the greatest Sufi teacher in India, Khwaja Moin-un-Din Chishti.[ix]

MOSES AND THE PEASANT BOY

There is a story told of Moses. One day he was passing through a farm, and he saw a peasant boy sitting quietly and talking to himself, saying "O God, I love you so; if I saw you here in these fields I would bring you soft bedding and delicious dishes to eat, I would take care that no wild animals could come near to you. You are so dear to me, and I so long to see you; if you only knew how I love you I am sure you would appear to me!" Moses heard this, and said, "Young man, how dare you speak of God in this way? He is the formless God, and no wild beast or bird could injure Him who guards and protects all." The young man bent his head sorrowfully and

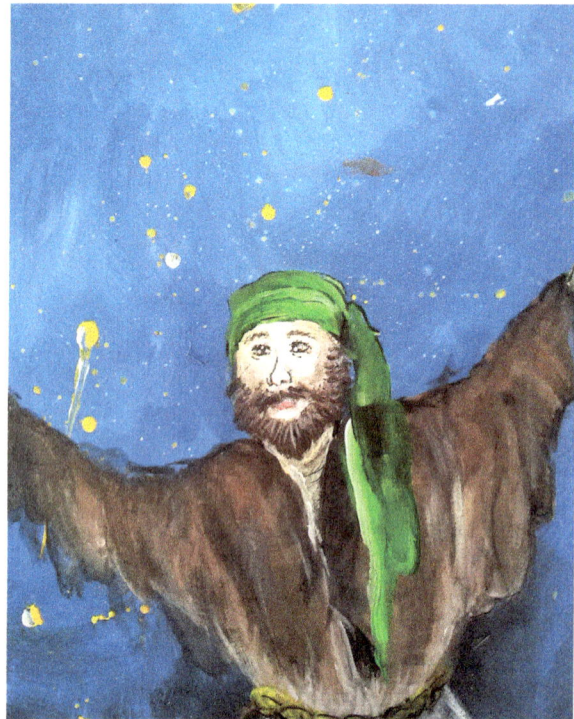

wept. Something was lost to him, and he felt most unhappy. And then a revelation came to Moses as a voice from within, which said, "Moses, what have you done? You have separated a sincere lover from Me. What does it matter what I am called or how I am spoken to? Am I not in all forms?"

This story throws a great light on this question, and teaches that it is only the ignorant who accuse one another of a wrong conception of God. It teaches us how gentle we ought to be with the faith of another; as long as he has the spark of the love of God, this spark should be slowly blown upon so that the flame may rise; if not, that spark will be extinguished.

How much the spiritual development of mankind in general depends upon a religious man! He can either spread the light, or diminish it by forcing his belief on others.[x] The God we know, or can know, is nothing but our conception, a picture that we have made of God for our own self, our own use. It is the greatest mistake for anyone to interfere with the conception of God held by another, or to think that another should have the same conception of God as he has himself. It is impossible.

Many different artists have painted the picture of Christ, yet each one is different. And since we allow every artist to have his own conception of Christ so we should allow every person to have his own conception of God.

We need not blame the ancient Chinese and Greeks and Indians who believed in many gods. Many gods is too small a number. In reality every single person has his own God. Besides all the different conceptions are really nothing but covers over one God.[xi]

A BRAHMIN AND AN ICONOCLAST

Someone once said to a Brahmin, "O foolish man, you have worshipped this idol for years. Do you think that it can ever answer you?" "Yes," said the Brahmin, "even from this idol of stone the answer will come if your faith is real. But if you have no real faith, you will get no answer even from the God in heaven." It is natural that man, who knows and sees all things through his senses and his feelings, and who tries to picture everything through his imagination, things that he has neither seen nor known, such as spirits, angels, and fairies, should make God intelligible to himself by means of his imagination.[xii]

LOST AT SEA

There is an Indian story about a fish which went to the Queen of the fishes and said, "I have always heard about the sea, but where is the sea?" Then the Queen explained to this fish who had come to her to learn, "You live, move, and have your being in the sea. The sea is within you and outside you, and you are made of sea and you will end in the sea. The sea is that which surrounds you and is your origin and your end and your own being."

Just as the fish was ignorant of the sea, so too may those who believe in the abstract be ignorant of its reality. One may stand near the water all one's life and yet remain thirsty, not realizing that it is water.

One day a man asked Buddha, "What is ignorance? You have spoken so often about it; can you illustrate it, can you explain it?" Buddha said, "There was a man who was clinging to the branch of a tree on a very dark night. All night he clung to that branch, and in the morning he saw that the ground was only one foot beneath his feet. And all the fear and anguish and torture he had felt throughout the whole night vanished with the breaking dawn."

Such is the nature of ignorance and reality. A person may continue to be unaware of the truth throughout his life and suffer all the consequences of this ignorance, for there is no greater misfortune than ignorance. One may continue to suffer one's whole life through ignorance, when the knowledge of reality is quite near if one only cared to find it.[xiii]

ONE LESSON, ONE LETTER

In the life of Bullah Shah, the great saint of Panjab, one reads a most instructive account of his early training when he was sent to school with boys of his own age. The teacher taught him *Alif*, the first letter of the Arabic alphabet. The other boys in his class finished the whole alphabet while he was mastering the same letter. When weeks had passed, and the teacher saw that the child did not advance any further than the first letter *Alif*, he thought that he must be deficient and sent him home to his parents, saying, "Your boy is deficient, I cannot teach him."

The parents did all in their power for him, placing him under the tuition of various teachers, but he made no progress. They were disappointed, and the boy in the end escaped from home, so that he should no longer be a burden to his own people. He then lived in the forest and saw the manifestation of *Alif* which has taken form in the forest as the grass, the leaf, the tree, the branch, the fruit, and the flower; and the same *Alif* was manifested as the mountain and hill, the stones and rocks; and he witnessed the same as a germ, an insect, a bird and a beast, and the same *Alif* in himself and others. He thought of one, saw one, felt one, realized one, and none else besides.

After mastering this lesson thoroughly he returned to pay his respects to his old teacher who had expelled him from school. The teacher, absorbed in the vision of variety, had long ago forgotten him; but Bullah Shah could not forget his old teacher who had taught him his first and most inspiring lesson which occupied almost all his life. He bowed most humbly before the teacher and said, "I have prepared the lesson you so kindly taught me; will you teach me anything more there may be to learn?" The teacher laughed at him and thought to himself, "After all this time this simpleton has remembered me." Bullah Shah asked permission to write the lesson, and the teacher replied in jest, "Write on this wall." He then made the sign of *Alif* on the wall, and it divided into two parts. The teacher was astounded at this wonderful miracle and said, "Thou art *my* teacher! That which thou hast learnt in the one letter *Alif*, I have not been able to master with all my learning," and Bullah Shah sang this song: Oh Friend! Now quit thy learning, / One Alif is all thou dost need. / By learning thou hast loaded thy mind, / with books thou hast filled up thy room. / But the true knowledge was lost by pursuing the false, / so quit now, oh friend, the pursuit of learning.

Every form seems to be derived from another, all figures being derived from *Alif*, which is originally derived from a dot and represents zero, nothingness. (In Arabic, zero is written as a dot.) It has nothingness which creates the first form *Alif*. It is natural for everyone when writing to make a dot as soon as the pen touches the paper, and the letters forming the words hide the origin. In like manner the origin of the One Being is hidden in His manifestation. That is why Allah, whose name comes from *Alif*, is hidden under His own manifestation. The same form of *Alif* is the figure one in English, and in both aspects this form reveals its meaning. This meaning in its various forms is seen in all aspects of nature.[xiv]

He that loveth not knoweth not God; for God is love.

– 1 John 4:8

"Blessed are the pure in heart, for they shall see God."

– Christ Jesus

In my soul there is a temple, a shrine, a mosque, a church where I kneel. Prayer should bring us to an altar where no walls or names exist.... In my soul there is a temple, a shrine, a mosque, a church that dissolve, that dissolve in God.

– Rabia Basri

MAJNUN & LEILA

The religious ideal is the medium by which one rises towards perfection. Whatever name a person gives to his ideal, that name is for him, and is most sacred to him. But this does not mean that giving it a name limits the ideal. There is only one ideal: the divine ideal. When someone said to Majnun, "Leila, your beloved, is not as beautiful as you think," he said, "My Leila must be seen with my eyes. If you wish to see how beautiful

Leila is, you must borrow my eyes."

Therefore if we wish to regard the object of devotion of whatever faith, of whatever community, of whatever people, we have to borrow their eyes, we have to borrow their heart. It is no use disputing over each historical tradition; they have often sprung from prejudice. Devotion is a matter of the heart, and is offered by the devotee.[vx]

MY MOTHER IS BEST

Some girls were playing one day, and each girl said in turn, "My mother is best." The others said, "No, my mother is best." And they were all arguing. But a girl among them who was wiser said, "Oh, no. It is the mother who is adorable, whether she be your mother or my mother."

The Sufi Movement does not interfere with anyone's ideal, nor with his devotion to his teacher; it would be as absurd as to think that a child should love another child's mother more than its own.

Therefore, we do not interfere with anybody's devotion to his teacher, but at the same time, the Sufi Movement invites souls to see the source and goal of all wisdom to be one and it is in this truth that all the blessing that the soul is longing for will be bestowed.[xvi]

THE CROWN JEWEL

There is a story told in the East of how a king was debating with his philosophers and friends on the question of wherein beauty lies. As they were talking together on the terrace of the palace they watched their children playing below in the courtyard. Suddenly the king called upon his slave, and handed him a jeweled crown, saying, "Take this and put it on the head of the child who best matches its beauty; choose and crown the most beautiful child in the courtyard." The slave, a little embarrassed, but pleased and interested, took the jeweled crown most carefully. First he tried it on the king's son; he saw that it suited the handsome lad and yet somehow the slave was not quite satisfied; there seemed to him something lacking about the child and he tried it on the head of another, and another, till at last he put it on the head of his own little son, and saw that it was a perfect fit; the crown became him wonderfully; it was just right! So the slave took his son by the hand, and leading him to the king, and trembling a little with fear said, "Sire, of all the children, I find that the crown suits this little one best. Indeed I must confess – although I am ashamed to appear so bold – that the boy is the son of my most unworthy self."

Then the king and those with him laughed heartedly as he thanked the slave and rewarded him with the same crown for his child, and said, "Certainly you have told me what I wished to know; it is the heart that perceives beauty." For the son of this slave was indeed a very ugly child, as the king and all those with him saw at a glance.[vxii]

And I will bring the blind by a way that they knew not; I will lead them in paths that they have not known: I will make darkness light before them, and crooked things straight. These things will I do unto them, and not forsake them.

– Isaiah 42:16

"For though the righteous fall seven times, they rise again; but the wicked are overthrown by calamity."

– King Solomon

I am in the ocean and an ocean is in me;
This is the experience of one who can see.
He that leaps into the river of Unity,
He speaks of union with his Beloved's beauty.

– Ahmad Jam

WALK ON WATER

There was a preacher who addressed some peasants, and he told them about a wonderful prayer which, when one repeated it, gave one the power to walk on water. One of the peasants was very interested in this prayer, and after saying it he walked across the river and back again, and he was very happy. So he went to this preacher and asked him in all humility to come and dine with him, he was so grateful for what the preacher had given him. The preacher accepted. And when he went to dine with the peasant there was a river to cross. The preacher said, "Where is the boat?" The man said,

"I have listened to your lesson, and since then I have not used my boat any more. We shall say the prayer and walk on water. Since you told me of it, that is what I have done." The preacher watched him doing it and felt ashamed. He had only talked about it; but now he realized that it is not knowing but believing that counts.

A thousand people may say the same prayer; but one person's prayer said with such faith and belief is equal to the prayers of a thousand people, because that prayer is not mechanical. Man is mechanical, and he generally says his prayers mechanically too. If he is genuine and if he has faith and belief and devotion, all he says has an effect; and that effect will perform miracles.

When we look at things from a mystical point of view we shall find that there is one single straight line, which is called aim. That line represents the line of the life of any being; the upper end is God, the lower end is man. The line is one. Though that line is one to the mystic and the philosopher in the realization of the truth, yet the line is unlimited at the upper end, and limited at the other. One end is immortality, the other is mortality.

The innermost yearning of life is to see the ends brought together. It is this prayer which draws the end which is man near to the end which is God. When he invokes the names of God man forgets his limitations and impresses his soul with the thought of the Unlimited, which brings him to the ideal of limitlessness. This is the secret of life's attainment.[xviii]

Triumph over anger with love. Triumph over evil with goodness. Triumph over malice with generosity. Triumph over lies with truth.

– Dhammapada

"The wise man is respectful to all who deserve respect, without discrimination" and "If you light a lamp for someone else it will also brighten your path."

– The Compassionate Buddha

My heart has become capable of every form: it is a pasture for gazelles and a convent for Christian monks, and a temple for idols and the pilgrim's Ka'ba and the tables of the Torah and the book of the Qur'an. I follow the religion of Love: whatever way Love's camels take, that is my religion and my faith.

– Ibn 'Arabi

A PATTERN MOST FAIR

There is a story told of Muhammad, that a man who had always maligned him and behaved as a bitter and treacherous enemy came to see him; and his disciples, hoping for revenge, were disappointed and indignant to find that Muhammad treated his despicable enemy with courtesy, even deference, granting his request. "Did you not see the gray in his beard?" asked Muhammad after the man had gone. "The man is old, and his age at least called for my courtesy."[xix] It is forgiveness and forbearance which recognizes the freedom and dignity of the human being that consumes all ugliness and burns up all unworthiness, leaving only beauty there.[xx]

The impermanent has no reality; reality lies in the eternal. Those who have seen the boundary between these two have attained the end of all knowledge. Realize that which pervades the universe and is indestructible; no power can affect this unchanging, imperishable reality. The body is mortal, but he who dwells in the body is immortal and immeasurable.

– Bhagavad Gita

"They are forever free who renounce all selfish desires and break away from the ego-cage of 'I,' 'me,' and 'mine' to be united with the Lord. This is the supreme state. Attain to this, and pass from death to immortality."

– Shri Krishna

If you wish to shine like the midday sun,
Burn up the darkness of self-existence.
Dissolve yourself in the Being of Him who is the Sustainer of all.
You have held fast to "I" and "we,"
And this dualism is your spiritual ruin.

– Rumi

DEATH BEFORE DYING

There is a story of a king who had a parrot which he loved so much that he kept it in a golden cage, and always attended to it himself. The king and queen both paid such great attention to the parrot that everyone in the palace was jealous of it. One day the king was about to go into the forest where the parrot came from, and he said to it, "My pet, I have loved you, and kept you with all the care and attention and fondness that I could; and I should like very much to take any message you wish to your brothers in the forest." The parrot said, "How kind of you to have offered to do this for me. Convey to

my brothers in the jungle that the king and queen have done their very best to make me happy: a golden cage, all kinds of fruits, and nice things of all sorts; and they love me so much. But in spite of all the attention they give me I long for the forest, and desire to dwell among you, free as I used to be before; this [thought] always possesses my mind. But I see no way out of if, so pray send me your goodwill and your love. One only lives in hope. Perhaps someday my wish will be granted." The king went into the forest, and approached the tree from which the parrot was taken and said to the brothers of the parrot, "O parrots, there is one whom I have taken from among you to my palace; and I am very fond of him, and he receives all the attention I can give. This is your brother's message." They listened to the message very attentively, and one after the other dropped to the ground and seemed to be dead.

The king was depressed beyond measure. Spellbound, he could not understand what it was that he had said that should have affected the feelings of those parrots so much. The loving parrots could not bear his message. And he thought, "What a sin I have committed, to have destroyed so many lives." He returned to his palace, and went to his parrot, and said, "How foolish, O parrot, to give me such a message that as soon as your brothers heard it, one after another, they dropped down, and all lay dead before me."

The parrot listened to this, and looked up gently to the sky, and then fell down too. The king was sadder than before. "How foolish I was! First I gave his message to them and killed them, and now I give their message to him and kill him also." It was almost bewildering to the king. What was the meaning of it all?

He commanded his servants to put his dead parrot on a golden tray, and bury him with pomp and ceremony. The servants took him out of the cage with great respect, and loosed the chains from his feet; and then, as they were laying him out, the parrot suddenly flew away and sat upon the roof.

The king said, "O parrot, you betrayed me." The parrot said, "O king, this was the aim of my soul, and it is the aim of all souls. My brothers in the jungle were not dead. I had asked them to show me the way to freedom, and they showed me. I did as they told me, and now I am free."

There is a chapter in the Qur'an which says: *Mutu qubla anta mutu*, which means, "Die before death." A poet says, "Only he attains to the peace of the Lord who loses himself." God said to Moses, "No man shall see Me and live." It means that when we see our being with open eyes, we see that there are two aspects to our being: the false and the true. The false life is that of this body and mind, which only exists as long as the life is within. In the absence of that life the body cannot go on. We mistake the true life for the false, and the false for the true.

Dying is this: when there is fruit or something sweet and good to taste, the child comes to its mother and says, "Will you give it to me?" Although it would have given pleasure to the mother to eat it, she gives it to the child. The eating of it by the child is enjoyed by the mother. That is death. She enjoys her life in the joy of another. Those who rejoice in the joy of another, though at their own expense, have taken the first step toward real life. If we are pleased by giving another a good coat which we would have liked to wear ourselves, if we enjoy that, we are on the first step. If we enjoy a beautiful thing so much that we would like to have it, and then give that joy to another, enjoying it through his experience, we are dead; that is our death; yet we live more than he. Our life is much vaster, deeper, greater.

Seemingly it is a renunciation, an annihilation, but in truth it is a mastery. The real meaning of crucifixion is to crucify this false self, and so resurrect the true self. As long as the false self is not crucified, the true self is still not realized. By Sufis it is called *fana*, annihilation. All the attempts made by true sages and seekers after real life are for the one aim of attaining to everlasting life.[xxi]

ACKNOWLEDGEMENTS

A number of people were instrumental to the creation of this book, most notably, the President of the Sufi Order International, Dr. Pir Zia Inayat-Khan, whose words of encouragement at the inception of this project and good faith in the compiler were a constant source of inspiration. Likewise, the former Secretary General of the Sufi Order International, Wahhab Sheets, has been a conduit of blessings, an invaluable mentor and guiding light. I also wish to acknowledge his wife, Batina, who helped find an appropriate quote from the Zoroastrian tradition for the Epigraph. Heartfelt gratitude is due to Suhrawardi Gebel as well, for providing the beautiful quote which appears in the Epigraph and References from the Buddhist tradition; and to Hafizullah Chishti, a most generous soul, for permitting me to use his winged-heart calligraphy (*Ya Hazrat-i 'Inayat – Qaddas Allahu Sirrahu*) featured on the title page.[22] All of our publications have been rendered flawlessly into print by our graphic designer, Sarah Carreck, to whom I am most grateful; and by my husband, Dr. Udaysinha Shinde, who has sustained this work through his love of spirituality and all things pure and true (*sattvic*). Last, but certainly not least, is the debt of gratitude I owe to the illustrator, Stephanie Reyes, for the sheer wonder that her artwork brings to this book and for her dedication and commitment to its realization.

REFERENCES

---

[i]   The noble Prophet Muhammad – may God's peace and blessings be upon him – said: "When a person dies, his deeds come to an end, except in respect of three matters which he leaves behind: a continuing charity (*sadaqat al-jariya*), knowledge from which benefit can be derived, and righteous children who will pray for him." (Narrated by Muslim, Tirmidhi and others.)

[ii]   "And the Tahagata addressed the venerable Kassapa, to dispel the uncertainty and doubt of his mind and he said: 'All things are made of one essence, yet things are different according to the forms which they assume under different impressions. As they form themselves so they act, and as they act so they are. It is, Kassapa, as if a potter made different vessels out of the same clay. Some of these pots are to contain sugar, others rice, others curds and milk; others still are vessels of impurity. There is no diversity in the clay used; the diversity of the pots is only due to the molding hands of the potter who shapes them for the various uses that circumstances may require. And as all things originate from one essence, so they are developing according to one law and they are destined to one aim which is Nirvana. Nirvana comes to thee, Kassapa, when thou understands thoroughly, and when thou livest according to

thy understanding, that all things are of one essence and that there is but one law. Hence, there is but one Nirvana as there is but one truth, not two or three,'" see Paul Carus, ed., "One Essence, One Law, One Aim," in *The Gospel of Buddha*. Heartfelt gratitude is due to Suhrawardi Gebel for providing this beautiful quote.

iii Prophet Zarathustra, the founder of Zoroastrianism, worshiped Ahura Mazda as the supreme, uncreated Being. In the Avestan language, Ahura Mazda means Wise Lord. Zoroastrianism proclaims that God is One and Lord of all, while accommodating worship of the One in many different aspects, with special emphasis being given to the sun and sun worship. According to Hazrat Inayat-Khan, the symbolic meaning of fire worship is the worship of the One Light that has no likeness, which is a mystical and theological belief found in almost all faith traditions. This imagery is vividly utilized by the Persian poet and Sufi saint Farid ad-Din Attar in *The Conference of the Birds*. Special thanks are due to Wahhab Sheets and his wife Batina, who found this quote from the Zoroastrian scriptures for the Epigraph.

iv This quote by Christ Jesus (peace be upon him) is analogous to an utterance attributed by Sufis to the Prophet of Islam (may a multitude of blessings be upon him): "I am Ahmad without the letter mim. I am an Arab without the letter 'ain. Who hath seen Me, the same hath seen the

Truth." Abu Bakr Siraj ad-Din has provided an illuminating commentary on the meaning of this highly esoteric statement in *The Book of Certainty: The Sufi Doctrine of Faith, Vision and Gnosis* (Cambridge: The Islamic Texts Society, 2010).

[v]   See: http://www.pirzia.org/writings/ten-sufi-thoughts/.

[vi]   Hazrat Inayat-Khan, *The Sufi Message: The Art of Personality* (Delhi: Motilal Banarsidass Publishers, 2011), 3:65.

[vii]   See: http://www.pirzia.org/writings/objects-of-the-order/.

[viii]   Pir Zia Inayat-Khan, *Caravan of Souls: An Introduction to the Sufi Path of Hazrat Inayat Khan* (New Lebanon: Suluk Press, 2013), 11-12.

[ix]   Hazrat Inayat-Khan, *The Inner Life* (Boston: Shambhala, 1997), 105-106.

[x]   Dr. H.J. Witteveen, ed., *The Heart of Sufism: Essential Writings of Hazrat Inayat Khan* (Boston: Shambhala, 1999), 59.

[xi]   Hazrat Inayat-Khan, *The Sufi Message: The Alchemy of Happiness* (Delhi: Motilal Banarsidass Publishers, 2002), 6:213.

[xii]   Dr. H.J. Witteveen, ed., *The Heart of Sufism: Essential Writings of Hazrat Inayat Khan* (Boston: Shambhala, 1999), 56.

[xiii]   Hazrat Inayat-Khan, *The Sufi Message: Philosophy, Psychology, Mysticism* (Delhi: Motilal Banarsidass Publishers, 2011), 11:18.

xiv Hazrat Inayat-Khan, *The Sufi Message: The Way of Illumination* (Delhi: Motilal Banarsidass Publishers, 2011), 1:40-41.

xv Hazrat Inayat-Khan, *The Sufi Message: The Unity of Religious Ideals* (Delhi: Motilal Banarsidass Publishers, 2009), 9:23 (slightly modified).

xvi Ibid., 9:271-272 (rearranged and slightly modified).

xvii Hazrat Inayat-Khan, *The Sufi Message: The Art of Personality* (Delhi: Motilal Banarsidass Publishers, 2011), 3:160 (slightly modified).

xviii Hazrat Inayat-Khan, *The Sufi Message: The Unity of Religious Ideals* (Delhi: Motilal Banarsidass Publishers, 2009), 9:51-52.

xix The Messenger of God (may blessings and peace be upon him) used to say: "He is not among us who does not respect the aged." He also said: "The best deed after belief in God is benevolent love towards people." And: "All creatures are the children of God, and the dearest to God are those who are most beneficial to His children."

xx Hazrat Inayat-Khan, *The Sufi Message: The Art of Personality* (Delhi: Motilal Banarsidass Publishers, 2011), 3:130.

xi Hazrat Inayat-Khan, *The Sufi Message: In an Eastern Rose Garden* (Delhi: Motilal Banarsidass Publishers, 2009), 7:185-187 (slightly modified).

xii For an explanation of this design, please visit Hafizullah Chishti's website: http://www.illuminedliving.com/wp-content/uploads/2012/11/the-winged-heart-calligraphy.pdf.

CPSIA information can be obtained
at www.ICGtesting.com
Printed in the USA
BVOW07s1335141216

470789BV00022B/247/P